CW01180373

NOTE TO PARENTS

This well known fairytale has been specially written and adapted for 'first readers', that is, for children who are just beginning to read by themselves. However, for those not yet able to read, then why not read this story aloud to your child, pointing to the words and talking about the pictures? There is a word list at the back of the book which identifies difficult words and explains their meaning in the context of the story.

Dick Whittington

retold by Pat Posner
illustrated by Gill Guile

Copyright © MCMLXXXVIII by World International Publishing Limited.
All rights reserved.
Published in Great Britain by World International Publishing Limited.
An Egmont Company, Egmont House,
P.O. Box 111, Great Ducie Street,
Manchester M60 3BL.
Printed in DDR.
ISBN 7235 8886 4

Once upon a time there was
a little boy called Dick Whittington.
Poor Dick had no mother
and no father.
He lived all on his own.

One day, an old man told Dick
about a place called London.
"In London, the pavements
are made of gold," said the old man.

"I am going to London
to see for myself," said Dick.
He put some food in a scarf.
Then he set off along the road.

Dick saw a farmer
from the next village.
"I will give you a lift in my cart,"
said the farmer.

In London, Dick looked everywhere for the streets of gold.
But he could not find any at all.

"I am so tired," sighed poor Dick.
"I will have a rest."
He fell fast asleep on a doorstep.
In the morning,
a man called Mr Fitzwarren
found Dick lying there.

"Cook needs someone
to help him," said Mr Fitzwarren.
"You can work in the kitchen."
But the cook was unkind.
Sometimes he hit Dick
with a rolling pin!

Dick was paid one penny
for the work he had done.
With his penny he bought a cat
at the market.
There were lots of mice
in the cold attic where Dick slept.
His cat would chase them away.

Dick loved his cat.
He called her Whiskers.
They were best friends.
Every night, Whiskers chased
the mice away.

One day, Mr Fitzwarren
called all his servants to him.
"One of my ships is sailing
to a faraway land," he said.
"You must all give the captain
something to sell for you."

"What will you give the captain?"
Alice asked Dick.
Alice was Mr Fitzwarren's daughter.
"All I have is Whiskers," said Dick.
"I will have to let the captain
take her to sell."

Dick felt very sad
without his best friend.
The mice came back to his room.
Dick did not like them.
He made up his mind to run away.

Just then the church bells
began to ring.
Dick could hear words!
"Turn again, Whittington,
Lord Mayor of London."
"They are talking to me!"
cried Dick. "I am turning back to
Mr Fitzwarren's house."

But what was happening
to Whiskers?
Well, the captain had taken her
to a faraway palace.
There were lots of mice there.
Whiskers chased them all away.

The queen asked to keep Whiskers.
"I will be very kind to Whiskers,"
the queen told the captain.
"The king will give you
lots of gold for her."

So the captain took the gold
and jewels in return for the cat.
When he left the palace, Whiskers
was sitting on the queen's lap.
Whiskers was purring,
so she must have felt happy.

The captain felt happy too.
He was sailing home and knew
Mr Fitzwarren would be pleased
with him.
He had sold all the goods.
Best of all, he had been given
gold and jewels for Whiskers.

As soon as the captain got home he hurried to see Mr Fitzwarren. "Look! The king and queen gave me all this for Dick's cat," he told Mr Fitzwarren.

Mr Fitzwarren called to one of his servants.
"Ask Mr Whittington to come here," he said.

"Look, Dick," said Mr Fitzwarren,
"your cat has made you very rich."
He gave Dick the gold and jewels.
"They *said* there was gold
in London," said Dick. "It was true!"

"You can pay a tailor,"
said Mr Fitzwarren,
"to make you some smart clothes."
So Dick sent for a tailor.

The tailor made some fine clothes.
Dick went to show them to Alice.
He looked very handsome indeed.
Alice fell in love with him.

Soon Dick and Alice were married.

Some years later, Dick Whittington became Lord Mayor of London.
He was so glad that he had heard the bells on that day long ago.
Do you remember what they said?

New words

Did you see a lot of new words in the story? Here is a list of some hard words from the story, and what they mean.

attic
a room at the very top of the house

captain
the boss of the ship

daughter
Alice was Mr Fitzwarren's little girl

everywhere
Dick looked all over the place

handsome
Dick was good looking

happening
what had Whiskers been doing?

jewels
very lovely stones